I Want to Be a
LION

by Thomas Kingsley Troupe
Illustrated by Melinda Beavers

"Josh, don't you want to see the lions?" my friend Omar asked.

I peeked down into their enclosure. A group of lions were resting in the sunshine.

"They look tired too," I said and yawned. "My baby brother kept everyone up last night."

"Oh, that's rubbish," Omar said. "Well, I'm going to take a closer look at these big cats."

"Good idea," I said. "I'll catch up in a minute."

"I want to be a lion," I mumbled as I closed my eyes. "Then I could sleep in peace."

I blinked, and everything changed. I stood on the bench and roared. I WAS a lion! I leaped into the enclosure to join the others.

I felt hot under all that fur. The sun made me feel even hotter. But finally I could sleep!

"Hey!" a lioness called to me. "You can't nap now! Watch the cubs while I hunt for some food for the pride."

4

Then suddenly the zoo enclosure disappeared. Tall grass waved as far as I could see. With no fences, I could run free forever. The zoo was nice, but it was nothing like the African savannah.

"Will you come and play with us?" asked one of the cubs.

I swatted at the cub and pretended to bite. I also kept watch for danger.

The lionesses attacked an antelope. It was over in seconds. The poor thing didn't stand a chance against those hunters.

I felt a fly land on my back. I used my tail to knock it away. It felt strange, as though I had an extra arm attached to my rear!

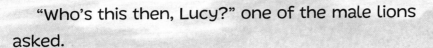

"Who's this then, Lucy?" one of the male lions asked.

"This is Josh," she said. "He's new to our pride."

The others nodded at me. All of the lions had short, light brown fur like mine, but the male lions also had large, dark manes.

Male lions can grow up to 3 metres (10 feet) long and can weigh up to 225 kilograms (500 pounds). Female lions can grow to almost 3 metres (9 feet) long and can weigh almost 180 kilograms (400 pounds).

"Let's eat," said one of the lions.

"Not so fast," Lucy said. "Here comes Snarl and his pride. They want our food."

The lions coming our way looked pretty tough. Lucy nodded towards them.

"Off you go, Josh," Lucy said. "Show them who's king of the savannah."

I ran towards Snarl, and he ran at me. I'd never moved so fast!

Sharp claws popped out of my paws. I swiped at Snarl and knocked him on the head. He scratched back. I opened my mouth to show Snarl my teeth.

Anger rose in my throat, and I let out a HUGE roar! The echo made it sound like ten angry lions.

Snarl and his pride left us alone. The lions in my pride seemed happy with me.

"Good work, Josh!" Lucy said. Her tail swished back and forth. "Time to eat!"

As the lions ate the antelope, I turned away.

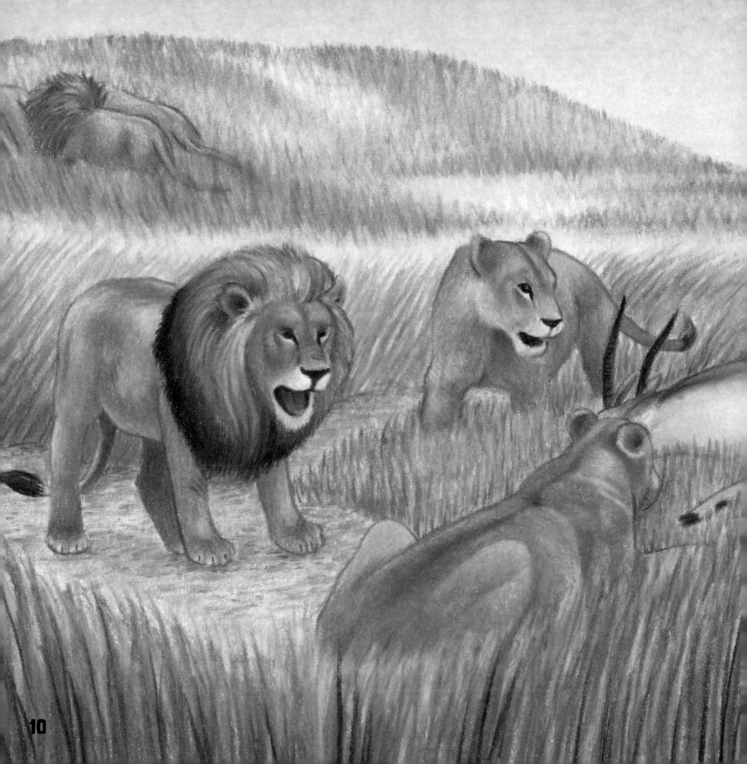

"What's the matter? Not hungry?" another male lion asked.

"Not really," I said.

"I'm tired of antelope," he said.

"Well, what else do you eat?" I asked.

"Oh, all sorts of things," the lion said. "Zebras, wildebeests, giraffes."

"Wow," I said. Suddenly I didn't want to eat ever again.

"If we're really hungry, we might even eat an elephant," he added.

I didn't know lions could attack something so big!

Lions don't always hunt a large prey. Sometimes they will eat smaller prey such as hares, birds or reptiles.

I watched a lioness with a rounded belly walk slowly away from the pride.

"Lilah is off to have her cubs," Lucy said. "She and the cubs won't return for a few months."

I looked around. I wondered where her mate was.

"Does she need someone to protect her?" I asked. "Or to help with the cubs?"

"In a group of lionesses, the mothers usually give birth around the same time," Lucy said. "They protect and nurse the cubs together."

"Wow! How many cubs will Lilah have?" I asked. Lilah's belly looked huge. There had to be six or seven cubs in there!

"Usually two or three," Lucy said. "They'll stay with Lilah until they're at least 2 years old."

I liked being part of the pride. The other lions wrestled around. Some of them licked each other's faces.

A little cub rubbed his head against my leg.

"Hello little one," I said. He growled to show he wanted to play.

"That's Jacques," Lucy said. "He's the laziest lion I know."

Jacques looked like he was dozing off. I was ready to snooze too.

"We all sleep a lot, but he's the king of naps," Lucy said.

Lions can sleep for up to 20 hours a day.

"Are those old lions?" I asked with a yawn. They moved a little slower than the rest.

"Yes," Lucy explained. "They're 10 or 11 years old. Most males live until they're about 12. Females usually live a few years longer."

"Whoa," I said, suddenly wide awake. "I'm going to be 12 in a few years!"

Lions live for up to 15 years in the wild and more than 20 years in captivity. Their biggest threats are from humans. People have taken over land where lions once lived. Also, some people hunt lions illegally.

Just then, we spotted some trucks coming towards us. Hunters with guns were in the trucks.

"Poachers!" one of the lionesses roared.

I leaped up. Lucy ran towards the trees, nudging the cubs along. Everyone ran away.

Almost everyone, I realized.

"Jacques!" I roared. I had to wake up that sleepy lion.

He stirred slightly as the trucks rumbled closer.

"Wake up!" someone else yelled.

"Wake up, Josh!" Omar shouted. I jumped up.

"I was just resting my eyes for a second," I said with a yawn.

"We're going to the next enclosure," Omar said. "C'mon!"

I stood and looked down into the lion enclosure. A lion that resembled Jacques yawned. It looked like it had just woken up too.

"So much for my cat nap," I said. I waved to my pride before I joined the rest of the class.

The African lion population has dropped by more than half in the last 30 years. Help to keep them from becoming extinct. Learn more about lions and support wildlife groups that help these, and other, amazing animals survive!

More about lions

- Male lions defend the pride's territory. That territory may be up to 260 square kilometres (100 square miles) of scrub or open grasslands.

- Lion cubs begin hunting when they are 11 months old.

- A lion roars to communicate with members of its pride and to warn other animals (including humans!) to stay away.

- When feeding on a large animal, a lion can eat almost 30 kilograms (65 pounds), and then won't need to eat again for several days.

- Lions live in prides of between 2 and 40 cats. The average pride has about 12 lions.

Glossary

extinct no longer living; an extinct species is one that has died out, with no more of its kind surviving

habitat natural place and conditions in which a plant or animal lives

horizon line where the sky and the earth or sea seem to meet

nurse drink mother's milk

poacher person who hunts or fishes illegally

population group of people, animals or plants living in a certain place

prey animal hunted by another animal for food

pride group or family of lions

reptile cold-blooded animal that breathes air and has a backbone; most reptiles lay eggs and have scaly skin

savannah flat, grassy area of land with few or no trees

territory area of land that an animal claims as its own to live in

Read more

Lazy Lion (African Animal Tales), Mwenye Hadithi (Hodder Children's Books, 1990)

Lion vs Gazelle (Predator vs Prey), Mary Meinking (Raintree, 2012)

Mighty Lions (Walk on the Wild Side), Charlotte Guillain (Raintree, 2014)

Websites

www.bbc.co.uk/nature/life/Lion
Find out more about lions – where they live, what they eat and how they behave. Look at stunning photographs and watch videos of lions in action.

http://gowild.wwf.org.uk/africa
Find out more about the African lion and other amazing African animals. Play games, read stories and make your own 3-D safari scene.

http://ngkids.co.uk/did-you-know/10-lion-facts
Find out more amazing lion facts and follow the links to make your own mighty lion!

Index

Books in this series

 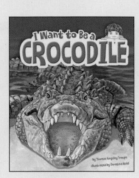  

Raintree is an imprint of Capstone Global Library Limited, a company incorporated in England and Wales having its registered office at 7 Pilgrim Street, London, EC4V 6LB – Registered company number: 6695582

www.raintree.co.uk
myorders@raintree.co.uk

Text © Capstone Global Library Limited 2016
The moral rights of the proprietor have been asserted.

Edited by Shelly Lyons and Nick Healy
Designed by Sarah Bennett
Creative Director: Nathan Gassman
Production by Tori Abraham

ISBN 978 1 4747 0420 5
19 18 17 16 15
10 9 8 7 6 5 4 3 2 1

British Library Cataloguing in Publication Data
A full catalogue record for this book is available from the British Library.

Acknowledgements
The illustrations in this book were created using coloured pencil with digital editing and effects.
The photograph on pages 20-21 are reproduced with permission of: Shutterstock/Volt Collection, page 21: Shutterstock/Adwo

We would like to thank Micaela Szykman Gunther, PhD, for her expterise, research and advice.

Every effort has been made to contact copyright holders of material reproduced in this book. Any omissions will be rectified in subsequent printings if notice is given to the publisher.

All the internet addresses (URLs) given in this book were valid at the time of going to press. However, due to the dynamic nature of the internet, some addresses may have changed, or sites may have changed or ceased to exist since publication. While the author and publisher regret any inconvenience this may cause readers, no responsibility for any such changes can be accepted by either the author or the publisher.

Printed in China.